With Fondest Love

To: _____

From: _____

Date: _____

How Do I Love Thee?

How Do I Love Thee?

A Romantic Gift of Love

Photographs by Orlando Marra

Conceived, designed, and styled by

JANA EMERICK

VIKING
STUDIO
BOOKS

❤ ❤ ❤

To Darrell with all my love
and In remembrance of my parents
for a wonderfully joyful,
loving childhood.

❤ ❤ ❤

VIKING
Published by the Penguin Group
Penguin Books USA Inc., 375 Hudson Street, New York, New York 10014, U.S.A.
Penguin Books Ltd, 27 Wrights Lane, London W8 5TZ, England
Penguin Books Australia Ltd, Ringwood, Victoria, Australia
Penguin Books Canada Ltd, 10 Alcorn Avenue, Toronto, Ontario, Canada M4V 3B2
Penguin Books (N.Z.) Ltd, 182-190 Wairau Road, Auckland 10, New Zealand
Penguin Books Ltd, Registered Offices:Harmondsworth, Middlesex, England
First published in 1995 by Viking Penguin, a division of Penguin Books USA Inc.
10 9 8 7 6 5 4 3 2 1

LIBRARY OF CONGRESS CATALOGING-IN-PUBLICATION DATA
How do I love thee?: a romantic gift of love/[compiled by] Jana Emerick; photographs
by Orlando Marra; photographs conceived, designed and styled by Jana Emerick.
p. cm.   ISBN 0–670–84056–4
1. Valentines—History—19th century. 2. Valentines—History—20th Century.
3. Calendar art. 4. Emerick, Jana—Art collections. 5. Greeting cards—Private
collection—New York (N.Y.) I. Emerick, Jana.
NC1866.V3H68 1994   741.6'84'09034—dc20   93–35918

The paper ephemera throughout this book is from The Jana Emerick Collection.
Printed in Singapore   Set in Berkeley Book   Designed by Virginia Norey

Acknowledgments

This book was inspired by love, and brought to fruition by the support and efforts of many special people whose valuable contributions are appreciatively recognized.

Heartfelt gratitude to the anonymous people who preserved and passed on their tokens of affection enabling us to enjoy their love-touched beauty.

For enriching and encouraging the study and appreciation of ephemera, the following organizations and institutions are to be acknowledged: the National Valentine Collectors Association, and its founder, Evalene Pulati; The Ephemera Society of America and its president, William F. Mobley; the American Antiquarian Society, Worcester, Mass.; The Metropolitan Museum of Art, N.Y.; the Museum of the City of New York; The New York Historical Society and the Cooper-Hewitt National Museum of Design, Smithsonian Institute, N.Y.

In recognition of their professionalism and for offering fine ephemera to me and other collectors, much

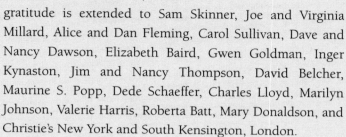

gratitude is extended to Sam Skinner, Joe and Virginia Millard, Alice and Dan Fleming, Carol Sullivan, Dave and Nancy Dawson, Elizabeth Baird, Gwen Goldman, Inger Kynaston, Jim and Nancy Thompson, David Belcher, Maurine S. Popp, Dede Schaeffer, Charles Lloyd, Marilyn Johnson, Valerie Harris, Roberta Batt, Mary Donaldson, and Christie's New York and South Kensington, London.

Special recognition is offered in loving memory of K. Gregory, Sarah Louise Tilton, and Elaine Skinner for their passionate love of valentines. I thank them for sharing this love with me.

Much appreciation to the following friends and family who each have contributed to this project in their own wonderful way: Ira Tilton, Jack and Becky Hogsed, Alex and Olga Emerick, James Kendrick, Peggy Hayes, Marion Rigo, Margaret Kelly, Carol Gray, Marjorie Cole, Ann Klein Fraser, Larry Young, Jackie Deval, Victoria Brown, Beverly Hofrichter, Jack Oshier, Larry Ellis, Ellen O'Neill, Jane Hirschkowitz, John De Luca, the late Ann Vargo, Mary Kovac, Gordon Beckhorn, Anne Schuster, Cindy Fox, Josephine Masters, and Kathleen La France.

Thanks to Valerie Bouhot-Regniault and Peter Genussa for greeting me with their warm smiles and cheerful assistance all those early mornings at the New York City flower market.

Much appreciation to Orlando Marra for his photographic

expertise and for the extra effort he expended to get the project done so proficiently.

Particular recognition and warmest thanks go to Rita Dubas for her commitment, valuable creative input, and styling assistance.

A very special thanks to Michael Fragnito, publisher of Viking Studio Books, for sharing my dream and guiding this book into a tangible token of affection to touch the hearts of many.

For their expertise and commitment to excellence I acknowledge the staff at Viking, most especially Barbara Williams, Kate Nichols, Virginia Norey, and my editor, Martha Schueneman.

Most significantly, I wish to recognize the quiet hero of this book, my dear husband, Darrell, whose special love, ingenious perceptions, and enthusiastic support bring so much joy and satisfaction to this project and all my endeavors.

An enduring tribute to the memory of the heart and soul of this book, my beloved parents, Michael and Anastasia (Nasta) Profant, whose special gifts of sensitivity, strength, love, and devotion were the impetus for this book.

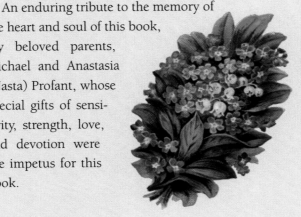

Introduction

♥

Love? I will tell thee what it is to love!
It is to build with human thoughts a shrine,
Where Hope sits brooding like a beauteous dove;
Where Time seems young—and Life a thing divine.
All tastes—all pleasures—all desires combine
To consecrate this sanctuary of bliss.
Above—the stars in shroudless beauty shine,—
Around—the streams their flowery margins kiss,—
And if there's heaven on earth, that heaven is surely this.

—CHARLES SWAIN

A special joy, unlike any other, prevails when we are in love. Life takes on a more magical quality, and our senses, emotions, and spirits soar to new heights. Sharing this euphoria with our beloved is a fundamental need; however, eloquently expressing the myriad emotions we feel is no simple task. There are so many wondrous thoughts and feelings to impart, yet they are so profound they seem inexplicable and far too dear to speak of in simple terms. Then, too, there is the question of knowing the right time and manner to express such tender endearments. This uncertainty can prompt a glib or clichéd communiqué, instead of the impassioned words we long to convey.

The resolution to this age-old quandary lies in observing how Victorians practiced the art of romance. During this era, unabashed romantic expression became an art form.

The Victorians perfected the enchanting ritual of exchanging love tokens. These cherished keepsakes were first bestowed by the gentleman to prove that his intentions were true, and gave the couple something to hold dear when not in each other's company.

Flowers were the most acceptable initial offering, and because each bloom conveyed a specific meaning, an intimate dialogue could be carried on through the "language of flowers." A gentleman could send a single bloom or bouquet to compliment his beloved's beauty or to declare his feelings. In return, the lady would reply with a floral token that expressed her thoughts. For the shy or uncertain suitor, this gracious medium of communication was a buffer from embarrassment or the possibility of unrequited love.

Handmade tokens of love were especially treasured and

were exchanged by lovers as their affinity for each other deepened. These mementoes came in every imaginable guise: Needlework, artwork, decorative watch papers, woven and cutwork paper hearts, or a lock of hair tied with a bow were the most popular.

Gifts of a more personal nature—a fancy handkerchief, floral scented sachet, an ornate pin cushion, a fan, jewelry, gloves and glove boxes, a photograph in a frame or locket, keepsake boxes, and books of love poems—were testaments of love presented by an ardent beau as the relationship intensified and the couple became engaged.

Love letters, laden with intimate revelations, were a favored means of interchange. These missives were held sacred, especially those in which intense emotions were expressed. Ladies often scented their letters with their signature perfume, adding an evocative personal touch to the declarations of love they wrote.

Poetry and song, both self-composed and borrowed from the masters, were a sensitive and seductive means of expressing the heart's fondest emotions. Many nineteenth-century suitors chose a romantic setting to recite tender words of love, in hopes that the surroundings would enhance the meaning of the words. Since the Victorians were so awe-struck by nature, a breathtaking landscape vista or an aromatic garden that intoxicated the senses were popular locations. A more cozy retreat by the warm glow of a fireplace also provided the perfect environment to ignite the flames of love. Such provocative surroundings often added a special magic when a fellow intended to propose.

Of all these displays of ardent affection, one stands out as the ultimate expression of love—the valentine. Imbued with all the romantic enticements one could fathom, the valentine, brought to its glory in the Victorian era, was love made manifest. Its sumptuous visual splendor and passionate declarations defined amorous emotion and made it the perfect gift of love.

The romantic legacy from a century ago, rich in sublime offerings of affection and charming courtship customs, stands as an inspiration to lovers today, perhaps because such overt sentimentalism and chivalrous deportment parallels our dreams of romance, and conveys the tender endearments we long to experience. Expressing your love in a similar manner could make the fantasy real.

In this treasury I have compiled sentimental tokens from that era of high romance, which express the many aspects of love, from the enchantment of first meetings to the deepening emotions of tenderness and adoration, and to the devotion found in everlasting love. An evocative array of poetry and song lyrics, paired with photographs filled with the beauty of heirloom valentines, tokens of love, and period finery from my collection, reflect the many moods and evolving stages of love.

It is my hope that you will find *How Do I Love Thee?* to be the perfect means of expressing your heartfelt feelings, and that the beautiful and alluring images and sentiments of distant times will echo the special words of love you long to say to the one you hold most dear.

Wishing you love's blessings,
Jana Emerick
New York City, 1995

With
Enchantment

♥ ♥ ♥

Love—it is the gift of Heaven,
Like the rose, how sweet its bloom,
And where'er is felt its presence,
There it dissipates each gloom.
And the heart that loveth truly,
In its first affection pure,
Shall, as long as life continues,
Find its happiness endure.

—VERSE FROM A LATE
19TH-CENTURY VALENTINE

$\mathcal{S}$OME ENCHANTED EVENING

Some enchanted evening
You may see a stranger,
You may see a stranger
Across a crowded room
And somehow you know,
You know even then
That somewhere you'll see her
again and again.

Some enchanted evening
Someone may be laughing,
You may hear her laughing
Across a crowded room
And night after night,
As strange as it seems
The sound of her laughter
will sing in your dreams.

Who can explain it?
Who can tell you why?
Fools give you reasons,
Wise men never try.

Some enchanted evening
When you find your true love,
When you feel her call you
Across a crowded room,
Then fly to her side
And make her your own,
Or all through your life
you may dream all alone.

Once you have found her,
Never let her go.
Once you have found her,
Never let her go!

—Lyrics by Oscar Hammerstein II
Music by Richard Rodgers

ℱIRST LOVE

I ne'er was struck before that hour
With love so sudden and so sweet,
Her face it bloomed like a sweet flower
And stole my heart away complete.

—JOHN CLARE

*F*AN FLIRTATION

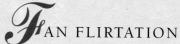

Carrying fan in right hand in front of face ....Follow me.

Carrying fan in left hand in front of face ....I wish to be acquainted.

Closing the fan...I wish to speak to you.

With handle to lips ....Kiss me.

Fan open wide ....Wait for me.

Drawing the fan across the cheek......................I love you.

For various purpose serves the fan,
    As thus—a decent blind,
Between the sticks to peep at man,
    Nor yet betray your mind.

Each action has a meaning plain,
    Resentment's in the snap,
A flirt expresses strong disdain,
    Consent a gentle tap.

All passions will the fan disclose,
    All modes of female art,
And to advantage sweetly shows
    The hand if not the heart.

'Tis folly's scepter first designed
    By love's capricious boy,
Who knows how lightly all mankind
    Are govern'd by a toy.

—ROBERT LLOYD FROM
THE CAPRICIOUS LOVERS

UNFORGETTABLE

💜 💜 💜

Unforgettable, That's what you are,
Unforgettable, Tho' near or far.
Like a song of love that clings to me,
How the thought of you does things to me,
Never before has someone been more
Unforgettable, in every way,
And forever more, that's how you'll stay.
That's why, darling, it's incredible,
That someone so Unforgettable
Thinks that I am Unforgettable, too.

—BY IRVING GORDON

With Adoration

♥ ♥ ♥

*L*ET ME CALL YOU SWEETHEART
(I'm In Love With You)

I am dreaming, dear, of you
Day by day
Dreaming when the skies are blue
When they're gray
When the silv'ry moonlight gleams
Still I wander on in dreams
In a land of love, it seems
Just with you:

Longing for you all the while
More and more
Longing for the sunny smile I adore
Birds are singing far and near
Roses blooming ev'rywhere
You alone my heart can cheer
You, just you:

Let me call you sweetheart, I'm in love with you
Let me hear you whisper that you love me, too
Keep the lovelight glowing in your eyes so true
Let me call you sweetheart, I'm in love with you.

—LYRIC BY BETH SLATER WHITSON
MUSIC BY LEO FRIEDMAN

ONE HEART'S ENOUGH FOR ME

One heart's enough for me—
    One heart to love, adore—
One heart's enough for me;
    O, who could wish for more?
The birds that soar above,
    And sing their songs on high,
Ask but for one to love,
    And therefore should not I?

One pair of eyes to gaze,
    One pair of sparkling blue,
In which sweet love betrays
    Her form of fairest hue;
One pair of glowing cheeks,
    Fresh as the rose and fair,
Whose crimson blush bespeaks
    The health that's native there.

One pair of hands to twine
    Love's flowers fair and gay,
And form a wreath divine,
    Which never can decay;
And this is all I ask,
    One gentle form and fair—
Beneath whose smiles to bask,
    And learn love's sweetness there.

—AUGUSTE MIGNON

The Bird in yonder cage confined,
Sings but to Lovers fond, sincere.

On wings of faith and hope, combined,
Brings soft emotion fondly dear.

*S*ince first I saw the light entrancing,
Now melting soft, now glowing bright,
That through thine eyes is ever glancing,
Telling of love and love's delight,
My heart no other joy has known,
Than love for Thee, and Thee alone.

—VERSE FROM A VALENTINE DATED 1895

A Valentine
to My Wife ~

She Was a Phantom of Delight

She was a phantom of delight
When first she gleamed upon my sight;
A lovely apparition, sent
To be a moment's ornament;
Her eyes as stars of twilight fair;
Like twilight's, too, her dusky hair;
But all things else about her drawn,
From May-time and the cheerful dawn;
A dancing shape, an image gay,
To haunt, to startle, and waylay.

I saw her upon nearer view,
A spirit, yet a woman too!
Her household motions light and free,
And steps of virgin liberty;
A countenance in which did meet
Sweet records, promises as sweet;
A creature not too bright or good
For human nature's daily food;
For transient sorrows, simple wiles,
Praise, blame, love, kisses, tears, and smiles.

And now I see with eye serene
The very pulse of the machine;
A being breathing thoughtful breath,
A traveller between life and death;
The reason firm, the temperate will,
Endurance, foresight, strength, and skill;
A perfect woman, nobly planned,
To warn, to comfort, and command;
And yet a spirit still, and bright
With something of an angel light.

—WILLIAM WORDSWORTH

With Romance

❤ ❤ ❤

You Decorated My Life

All my life was a paper, once plain, pure and white;
till you moved with your pen, changin' moods
   now and then
till the balance was right;
Then you added some music, Every note was in place;
And anybody could see all the changes in me
by the look on my face;

And you decorated my life;
Created a world, where dreams are a part
And you decorated my life,
by painting your love all over my heart;
You decorated my life.

Like a rhyme with no reason, in an unfinished song,
There was no harmony, life meant nothin' to me,
until you came along;
And you brought out the colors; What a gentle surprise;
Now I'm able to see all the things life can be
shinin' soft in your eyes;

And you decorated my life;
Created a world, where dreams are a part
And you decorated my life,
by painting your love all over my heart;
You decorated my life.

—By Debbie Hupp and Bob Morrison

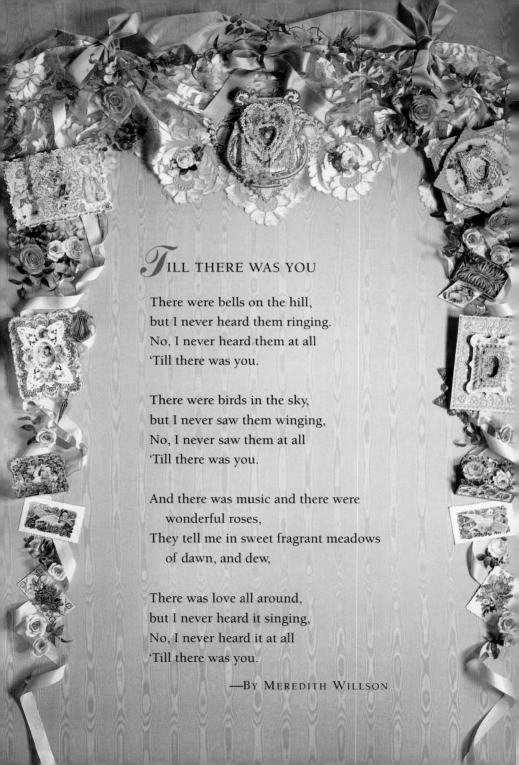

TILL THERE WAS YOU

There were bells on the hill,
but I never heard them ringing.
No, I never heard them at all
'Till there was you.

There were birds in the sky,
but I never saw them winging,
No, I never saw them at all
'Till there was you.

And there was music and there were
  wonderful roses,
They tell me in sweet fragrant meadows
  of dawn, and dew,

There was love all around,
but I never heard it singing,
No, I never heard it at all
'Till there was you.

—BY MEREDITH WILLSON

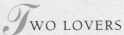WO LOVERS

Two lovers by a moss-grown spring;
    They leaned soft cheeks together there,
    Mingled the dark and sunny hair,
And heard the wooing thrushes sing.
      O budding time!
      O love's blest prime!

—GEORGE ELIOT

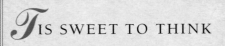

'TIS SWEET TO THINK

❧

The heart, like a tendril,
    accustomed to cling,
Let it grow where it will,
    cannot flourish alone,
But will lean to the nearest and
    loveliest thing
It can twine with itself, and make
    closely its own.

—THOMAS MOORE

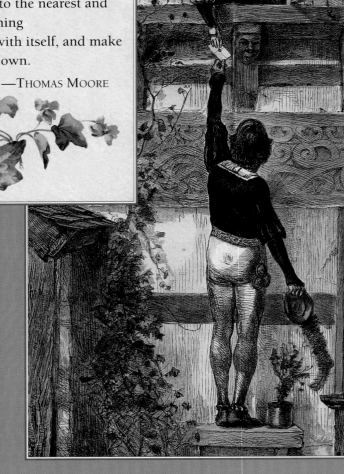

here is a spell that o'er the mind
A veil of varied beauty throws,
That gives a music to the wind,
And adds e'en perfume to the rose.
This joyous state, this blissful dream,
That lifts us the dull world above,
Flinging its halo on Life's Stream,
This magic power is happy Love.

—VERSE FROM AN
1840'S VALENTINE

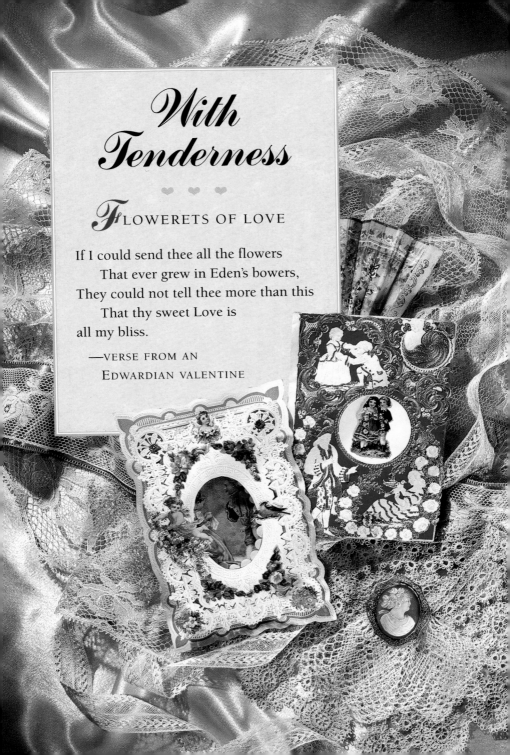

With Tenderness

♥ ♥ ♥

*F*LOWERETS OF LOVE

If I could send thee all the flowers
    That ever grew in Eden's bowers,
They could not tell thee more than this
    That thy sweet Love is
all my bliss.

    —VERSE FROM AN
    EDWARDIAN VALENTINE

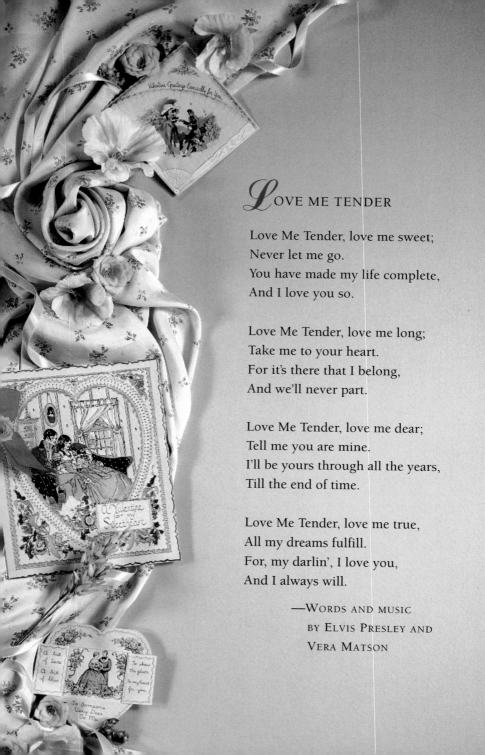

*L*OVE ME TENDER

Love Me Tender, love me sweet;
Never let me go.
You have made my life complete,
And I love you so.

Love Me Tender, love me long;
Take me to your heart.
For it's there that I belong,
And we'll never part.

Love Me Tender, love me dear;
Tell me you are mine.
I'll be yours through all the years,
Till the end of time.

Love Me Tender, love me true,
All my dreams fulfill.
For, my darlin', I love you,
And I always will.

—WORDS AND MUSIC
BY ELVIS PRESLEY AND
VERA MATSON

Then do not turn thy heart away
No longer let me pine
But let to-morrow be the day.
Of bliss - and Valentine

T. Richardson Derby.

$\mathcal{T}$ENDERLY

The evening breeze caressed the trees
    Tenderly;
The trembling trees embraced the breeze
    Tenderly.
Then you and I came wandering by
And lost in a sigh were we.

The shore was kissed by sea and mist
    Tenderly.
I can't forget how two hearts met breathlessly.
Your arms opened wide and closed me
    inside;
You took my lips, you took my love so
    Tenderly.

—LYRIC BY JACK LAWRENCE
MUSIC BY WALTER GROSS

THE EVENING TIME

Together we walked in the evening time,
Above us the sky spread golden and clear,
And he bent his head and looked in my eyes,
As if he held me of all most dear.
    Oh! it was sweet in the evening time!

Grayer the light grew and grayer still,
The rooks flitted home through the purple shade;
The nightingales sang where the thorns stood high,
As I walked with him in the woodland glade.
    Oh! it was sweet in the evening time!

And our pathway went through fields of wheat;
Narrow that path and rough the way,
But he was near and the birds sang true,
And the stars came out in the twilight gray.
    Oh! it was sweet in the evening time.

Softly he spoke of the days long past,
Softly of blessed days to be;
Close to his arm and closer I prest,
The cornfield path was Eden to me.
    Oh! it was sweet in the evening time!

And the latest gleams of daylight died;
My hand in his enfolded lay;
We swept the dew from the wheat as we passed,
For narrower, narrower, wound the way.
    Oh! it was sweet in the evening time.

He looked in the depths of my eyes, and said,
"Sorrow and gladness will come for us, sweet;
But together we'll walk through the fields of life
    Close as we walked through the fields of wheat."

—A.C.C.

With
Devotion

How do I love thee?
   Let me count the ways.
I love thee to the depth
   and breadth and height
My soul can reach,
   when feeling out of sight

For the ends of
   Being and ideal Grace.
I love thee to the level
   of everyday's
Most quiet need,
   by sun and candlelight.

—ELIZABETH BARRETT BROWNING

THE VALENTINE

Devoted to You

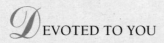

❤ ❤ ❤

Darling, you can count on me till the sun
    dries up the sea
Until then I'll always be devoted to you.
I'll be yours thru end-less time,
I'll adore your charms sublime.
Guess by now you know that I'm devoted
    to you.
I'll never hurt you, I'll never lie,
I'll never be untrue
I'll never give you reason to cry,
I'd be unhappy if you were blue
Thru the years my love will grow,
like a river it will flow
It can't die because I'm so devoted to you.

—Words and music by
Boudleaux Bryant

*D*earest of creatures to thee I send
this knot of love which hath no end
To let you know my love is true
and that to none alive but you
Therefore my humble mind is bent
Fail not my love to give consent
To be my love and live with me
As long as life shall granted be
Then let us unite our hearts in twain
never more to part again.

—VERSE FROM ENDLESS KNOT OF LOVE,
CIRCA 1800, PICTURED ABOVE

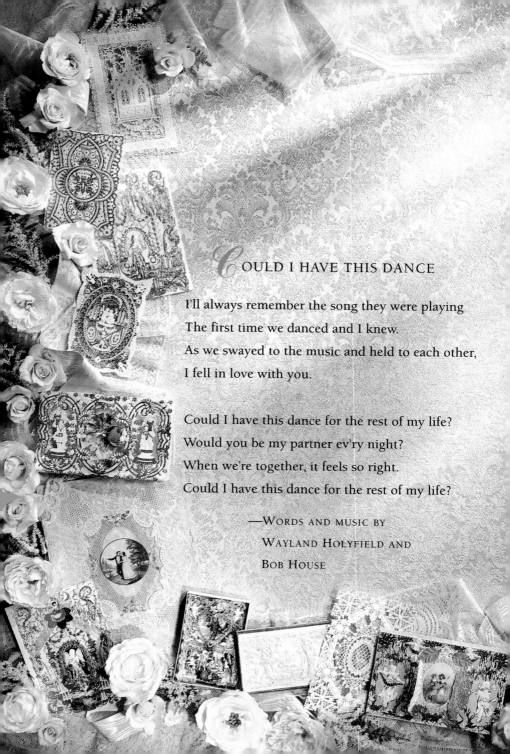

COULD I HAVE THIS DANCE

I'll always remember the song they were playing
The first time we danced and I knew.
As we swayed to the music and held to each other,
I fell in love with you.

Could I have this dance for the rest of my life?
Would you be my partner ev'ry night?
When we're together, it feels so right.
Could I have this dance for the rest of my life?

—WORDS AND MUSIC BY
WAYLAND HOLYFIELD AND
BOB HOUSE

Notes

Pages 1 and 3–7: During the nineteenth century, technological advances in chromolithography, die-cutting, and embossing made it possible to produce the array of stunning late–Victorian "die-cuts" that embellish these pages.

Cover and Page 2 (opposite title page): This late-1890's double-tiered paper-lace valentine, stunningly detailed with silvered paper lace, applied scraps, and embossed gilded floral background, is an especially romantic tribute to love.

Page 8: A daintily detailed silhouette picture from the 1930's, stenciled on glass.

With Enchantment

Pages 12 & 13: These intricately ornamented, embossed, and perforated paper-lace valentines including two silver lace sachets, date from the "golden era" of valentines, 1840–1870. In 1834, Englishman Joseph Addenbrooke discovered the process for lace paper making, which enabled such lacy wonders to be conceived and executed.

Page 15: The romantic eighteenth-century scene of a courtly eighteenth century gentleman presenting a floral tribute to his lady fair is elegantly rendered in this late 1890's foldout valentine created by the royally appointed English firm, Raphael Tuck and Sons, Ltd.

Pages 16 & 17: A myriad of fan tokens of affection, circa 1880 to 1910, are reminiscent of a time when the fan was a symbol of gentility and grace, as well as a requisite implement for artful flirtation.

Page 18: A pair of unforgettable tiered paper-lace valentines, circa late 1870's–early 1880's, are presented as portraits framed in filigree. The top valentine is by Esther Howland, the one below by George Whitney, who bought out Miss Howland's company around 1881. Mr. Whitney and other American valentine manufacturers closely emulated her tiered lace style through the turn of the century.

Page 19: Love's enchantments are tenderly expressed in these cherished keepsakes. The top gilded, tiered paper-lace valentine, circa 1880, and the bottom miniature valentine, circa 1870's, are by

Taft. The gilded cameo sachet paper lace folder and cameo embossed paper-lace valentine of a couple in Cupid's garden, as well as the pink, seashell cameo paper-lace valentine are all Esther Howland's creations from the 1860's.

With Adoration

Pages 20 & 21: These charming valentines, postcards and gifts from 1895–1910 are filled with adoring sentiments meant for a special sweetheart.

Page 22: A turn-of-the-century sweetheart wall hanging with illustrations by Frances Brundage is coupled with a floral collage attended by a pretty crepe-paper-skirted Victorian paper doll.

Page 23: This beautifully embellished 1875 English valentine is an endearing expression of adoration. Its silvered seafoam green embossed perforated paper lace is enhanced with gathered pleated mesh centered around a scrap of a loving angelic couple.

Page 24: Originally created by Joseph Addenbrooke in the 1830's, this valentine is from the "Unrequited Love" series. The series is made up of a set of fourteen, each depicting a different aspect of love. The central picture is a hand-colored aquatint with an embossed border surrounding it.

Page 25: This elaborately embossed English valentine, dated February 14, 1853, would have swept any lady off her feet. Inside is a hand-written love poem.

Page 26: The idealized grace and gentility of images from the eighteenth and nineteenth centuries were a favorite theme of greeting cards in the 1930's. This sublime valentine from the late 1930's shows a genteel Victorian lady richly adorned in crimson and lace, hinting that the same elegance is possessed by the recipient of this card.

With Romance

Pages 28 & 29: Indicative of the ostentation of the Gilded Age, these lavish multi-layered late Victorian valentines are built up in tiers that consist of paper lace and lithograph layers supported by paper springs. They are further embellished with scraps and other decorations such as satin ribbons.

Page 30: Late Victorian and Edwardian tiered lace valentines and late 1900's hidden-name visiting cards are intermingled with a sterling silver visiting card case and jewelry of the era.

Page 31: This photo depicts the romance of a leisurely afternoon picnic, at the turn of the century, when love as gentle as a breeze was expressed in poetry and sumptuous affectionate offerings, such as this tiered lace valentine, dated 1902.

Page 32: A hand-colored engraving from *Harper's Weekly* dated February 24, 1877, shows the exchange of a missive on St. Valentine's Day in merry old England.

Page 33: Entwined in ivy, symbolic of fidelity, these classic examples of American tiered lace valentines (circa late 1870's to late 1880's) are from George Whitney, whose company created valentines from the 1860's to 1942.

Page 34: A quiet moment steeped in the sentiment of enjoying a collection of beautiful hand-colored valentines from the 1930's.

Page 35: The luxurious and romantic connotations of lace are represented in this photo featuring a circa 1855 embossed silvered paper-lace valentine by Mansell, displayed upon a handmade Victorian lace table scarf.

With Tenderness

Page 36: Tender loving sentiments are vividly expressed in the majestic splendor of this paper lace and lithograph tiered valentine dated 1900.

Page 37: Lacy confections such as these evoke the sentimentality of a century ago. The two valentines pictured here are quite special because they are the work of Esther Howland, pioneer in the field of lace-paper valentine design in America. The valentine on the right (circa 1860's), is made of gilded cameo embossed paper lace backed in a vivid blue with applied scraps. On the left is Miss Howland's classic style (circa 1873–1880) of using tiered paper lace, applied scraps, and brightly colored paper disks behind the lace at the corners.

Page 38: Hand-colored valentines from the 1930's are swathed in a rose print fabric of the era.

Page 39: Elegant tokens of esteem and valentines (circa 1850–1900) are presented as offerings of love. The background print (chromolithograph circa 1890's) shows a fashionable lady of the era relishing treasures perhaps sent by a smitten beau.

Page 40: The stunning engraved wood border of this 1840's valentine enhances the tender scene of love in bloom, pictured in the hand-colored lithograph.

Page 42: Featuring two rare Civil War tent valentines and a love letter from a Union soldier dated February 20, 1863, this vignette is a poignant homage to love. The tent opens to reveal a soldier reminiscing about his sweetheart. The miniature sword is a letter opener, and the photo and frame are of the period.

With Devotion

Page 44: A circa 1790's handmade "puzzle purse" sits partly open as if it had just been penned by an admirer. To decipher the message of love, unfold and read the puzzle in numerical order. As an added surprise, a love token or ring might have been hidden inside. The size of this piece, when fully open, is 12.5 inches square.

Page 46: This late-nineteenth century chromolithograph print, titled "The Valentine," illustrates how passionately Victorians felt about receiving such a missive.

Page 48: Endowed with love and tenderly treasured through time are these eighteenth- and early nineteenth-century handmade keepsakes. Included in this montage are a woven paper double heart, a woven paper heart pocket which often held a love token, three lock-of-hair tokens, an acrostic valentine (center), and, in the upper right, a rare early eighteenth-century hand-colored cut-work token of friendship and love made by nuns, and sold for the benefit of charity.

Page 49: A hand-penned and cut-work "endless-knot-of-love" proposal, circa 1800, of Pennsylvania origin, is displayed upon a doll's quilt of the same century. The remarkable hand-crafted workmanship of both pieces is enhanced when played against each other.

Page 50: Masterful workmanship is evident in these "cameo lace" valentines, lace paper "blanks," and embossed boxed valentine, circa 1860's–1870's. In the lower left corner is an earlier quarto size valentine of perforated lace (late 1840's) with the center medallion cut out to show a hand-colored scene of a romantic couple, through sheer silk mesh.

Page 51: When an attached string is lifted on the delicate tissue paper cut-work of this "cobweb" or "beehive" valentine, a hand-colored scene of a couple dancing is revealed. This English perforated paper-lace fantasy by Addenbrooke is dated 1845.

Special Credits and Acknowledgments

The author and publisher would like to thank everyone who granted the necessary permissions to reproduce song lyrics and cards including the following:

Norcross, Inc., Rust Craft Greeting Card Co., Inc., Marvin A. Rosenblum, Chairman of the Board: page 34, Standing upper left, sweetheart valentine with hand-coloring, silvered border, and attached coral satin ribbon; circa 1935. Page 38, valentine center, hand-colored with gilt detailing, and attached coral satin ribbon; circa 1935.

"Some Enchanted Evening" by Richard Rodgers, Oscar Hammerstein II. Copyright © 1949 by Richard Rodgers and Oscar Hammerstein II. Copyright Renewed. WILLIAMSON MUSIC owner of publication and allied rights throughout the world. Used by Permission. International Copyright Secured. All Rights Reserved. Lyric on page 14.

"Unforgettable" words and music by Irving Gordon. © Copyright 1951 (renewed) by Bourne Co. All Rights Reserved. International Copyright Secured. Lyric on page 18.

"Let Me Call You Sweetheart" by Leo Friedman and Beth Slater Whitson. Copyright © 1910 (renewed) Paull-Pioneer Music. International Copyright Secured. All Rights Reserved. Used by permission of Shawnee Press, Inc. (ASCAP) and Shapiro, Bernstein & Co., Inc. Lyric on page 21.

"You Decorated My Life" by Debbie Hupp and Bob Morrison. © 1978 TEMI COMBINE INC. All Rights Controlled by MUSIC CITY MUSIC, INC. and Administered by EMI APRIL MUSIC INC. (ASCAP). All Rights Reserved. International Copyright Secured. Used by Permission. Lyric on page 29.

"Till There Was You" from "The Music Man." By Meredith Willson. © 1950, 1957 (renewed) FRANK MUSIC CORP. and MEREDITH WILLSON MUSIC. All Rights Reserved. Used by Permission. Lyric on page 30.

THANKS AND APPRECIATION are extended to the following people and establishments who have graciously loaned their treasures to be included as props in the following photos:

- Classic Designs, Ltd.   (203) 598-0333
  One-of-a-kind design straw hat; page 31.
- Doris Zall   (212) 749-7060
  Brass 1930's colonial lady pendant, vintage lace heart pillow and tulle lace sham; page 34. Sterling silver calling card case, umbrella, and lyre pins and sterling filigree necklace; page 30. Gentleman's Victorian card case; page 45. Tapestry, page 14.
- John Koch Antiques   (212) 243-8625
  Nineteenth century butlers desk; pages 44 and 45.
- René Inc.   (212) 860-7669
  Silver-plate tea caddy, tray, and teaspoon; page 34.
- Treasures From The Past / Antiques by Dorene Inc.   (201) 243-0522
  Circa 1860's partners ink well set and circa 1880 wooden dome top letter chest with brass hardware; pages 44 and 45. Gold-filled early 1900's filigree cameo pin; page 37. Circa 1910 hand-painted porcelain pins; pages 20 and 39.

*J*ana Emerick is the owner of J.P. Emerick Collectables, a shop and design firm that specializes in Victoriana, romantic gifts, and decorative accessories. A free-lance writer, designer, and stylist, Ms. Emerick also teaches workshops and lectures on nineteenth-century social history, decorative arts, and crafts at such places as The *Forbes* Magazine Galleries; the Cooper-Hewitt, National Museum of Design, Smithsonian Institution; the Museum of the City of New York; Parsons School of Design, New York; and for The Victorian Society in America, Metropolitan Chapter. Her work has been featured nationally in articles through the Associated Press. Ms. Emerick divides her time between Atlanta and Manhattan, where she lives with her husband.